Improve Your Marriage
31 Days In
31 Ways

Improve Your Marriage
31 Ways In
31 Days

Dr. Tony Lester

Rush House Books Publishers, Austin, Texas

Copyright © 2010 by Dr. Tony Lester

Published in the Austin, Texas, by Rush House Books

Cover image by Rush House Books

Scriptures quotations are taken from the New King James Version (NKJV).

All rights reserved. Written permission must be secured from the author to use or reproduce any part of this book except for grief quotations in critical reviews or articles. No part of this publication may be reproduced, stored in a retrieval system, or transmitted, in any form or by any means, including electronic, mechanical, photocopying, recording, or otherwise without prior written permission.

Lester, Dr. Tony
Improve Your Marriage/31Days In 31 Ways
ISBN 9780615454610
1. Marriage 2. Christian

ACKNOWLEDGEMENTS

Special thanks to my wife, Dana Lester; daughter, Kay Nicole Lester; mother, Barbara Butler; father, Pastor Greg Butler; grandmother, Miriam Haynes; for making this book possible.

Tony

The Author

There is a select group of people who are called to deliver the Word of God to a society transitioning from lost lambs to devout Christians. Of those chosen few God has called Dr. Tony Lester to mesmerize a demographic in need of spiritual restoration. In contrast to other ministers who simultaneously lecture and preach, Dr. Tony Lester's down-to-earth approach fumigates the confessional fear in people to express their problems openly. His accessible personality and humorous nature makes him the perfect candidate to reach millions in their darkest hour. These qualities plus sheer determination and an unconditional love for God ignited a desire to share his testimony. Dr. Lester earned a Doctorate in Theology from the Andersonville Theological Seminary.

Preface

When men and women get married, their wedding day is the beginning of a life together. They are so happy and full of joy. It becomes the best day of their lives. For many couples, the joyful months or years pass, and the church becomes a courtroom, the minister becomes a judge, and the love and joy are replaced by bitterness and hatred. The state laws on divorce replace the biblical vows of marriage. Their day in court becomes the worst day of their lives. What happened?

The first couple of years after my wife and I were married, we argued a lot. It wasn't because of a lack of love or money, we just argued about anything and everything. I can remember one day I asked God, "Why are my wife and I arguing so much?" The Holy Spirit told me, *"Because no one taught you how to be a husband, and no one taught her how to be a wife. So you and your wife are just winging it."*

See, I thought being a husband meant having a job, good sex, fixing things around the house, taking out the trash, and being the leader of the house. It seemed pretty simple to me. When I got married I found that there were several things I left out like being a good listener; telling my wife how much I appreciated her; telling her how beautiful she looked; asking her how her day went; and telling her thank you, please, you're welcome, and I love you. Little things like these have a big impact.

I

In my years of counseling and experiences within my own marriage, I felt an easy-to-follow daily guide to help protect marriages against divorce was an important need. In thirty-one days, couples can read and discuss the elements of their marriages. My wife, Dana, and I pray that your marriage will be strengthened each day, as ours has been.

Introduction

The Book of Genesis is not just the introduction of God and mankind; it's also the beginning of marriage. This is a very crucial moment in time and history. The time is crucial because God told Adam to "be fruitful and multiply, and fill the earth." The history was crucial because this is the first order God gave man. Adam needed a woman companion to obey God.

God made marriage the moral way to have sex. In order for Adam to have sexual relations with Eve, she first came to be his wife. And *[Jesus] answered and said to them "Have you not read that He who made them at the beginning made them male and female," and said, "For this reason a man shall leave his father and mother and be joined to his wife, and the two shall become one flesh? So then, they are no longer two but one flesh. Therefore what God has joined together, let no man separate"* (Matthew 19:4-6).

Jesus taught these words to a religious society that had low regard for the sacred relationship of marriage, as instituted by God. His words ring true to our society today. You and your mate came to God and society witnessed this. When some people get a divorce they are telling God the same thing that Adam told him, "The mate you gave me caused me to sin." At least when Adam blames God it was a legitimate accusation. Adam went to sleep alone and woke up to Eve. Adam didn't have a choice in his mate. When Abraham sent his servant to get a wife for Isaac, he brought back Rebecca. Isaac had a choice. He could have refused her and married another woman, but he didn't. Why? Because he knew that God knew which mate was best for him.

God will bring a mate to us, but it's up to us to choose that person. When some people get a divorce, they tend to blame God. "God ordained the marriage—not the mate." This means that God doesn't bless a mate; he blesses the marriage (which is *two* individuals). When some people get a divorce, it's because they can't get along with their mate. God did not choose your mate. You did!

In some divorces, people act foolishly, as if they are losing their minds. They attack their mate, their marriage (and thus, God), and will say, "The best thing for us is to get a divorce." Wrong answer. God says, "That is the worst thing you can do for your marriage."

Divorce

There are many spouses who have disagreements with their mate, but the marriage is innocent. The divorcee would say something like, "My mate sucks (that may be true), and this marriage is not working (this is not true)." The marriage is working because it has *"obtains favor from the Lord"* (Proverb 18:22). You and your mate are not working. Some people get a divorce for one reason and one reason alone—they want to! God blesses marriages, and when you get a divorce you curse it. Separation is better than divorce; sometimes people need to back off for a minute or two but not for a lifetime.

You can think of your toughest job, and it would not come close to a day in a bad marriage. There are people who divorce for the same reason they would leave a job. What if you got a job but didn't bother to look over the job description? You get to work, and you are doing everything but what you thought you would do. The first thought that comes to your mind is, "I am leaving because I did not sign up for this! This is not the way I thought it will be." This is the same problem that we have in some marriages today. Every married person has felt like this at one time or another, and the couples that read the job description (the Bible, good marriage books, seminars or events, and older couples as mentors) work through it. Too many people go into a marriage with their personal opinion of marriage, and when things don't work out the way they planned, they leave. After years of debating and living in holy matrimony, you decide that your mate is the child of the devil. The only thing left for you to do is to divorce him or her. Your mind tells you, "Don't feel bad about it. You had no other choice." This is a lie! You *do* have a choice; divorce is the easy way out. You may say, "I don't know him or her, and he or she is a mean person." Maybe, but you didn't think he or she was mean when you married. So maybe you turned him or her into a mean person.

Let's look back at the story of Adam and Eve. First, we would start with Adam and Eve in the garden. The serpent spoke to Eve about sinning against God. Eve was deceived and ate from the tree of the knowledge of good and evil. The only time you hear about Adam in this story is after Eve ate the fruit and passed it to him. Let's stop right there. Where was Adam at this crucial moment when the serpent was talking to Eve?

Doing his thing (whatever his thing is)?
Working?
Watching the Super Bowl?
At Corey's or Pam's house?
Sleeping?
Preaching?

The Bible doesn't tell us where Adam was, but it does tell us what Adam did (sin against God and blame Eve and God). The man was supposed to watch and guard the garden and everything in it. I understand what Adam was saying when he told God it was not his fault: "I was working hard in this garden, having good sex, fixing things around the garden, taking out the trash, and being the leader in the garden. And this lady that I am married to is cheating on me the whole time with a snake. I did not sign up for this, and this is not the way I thought it would be. Therefore I am leaving."

The main point in the story about Adam and Eve was disobedience. First, Eve sinned against God, and then Adam did. This seems like some of the marriages now. One mate cheats, the other finds out, and then they both cheat. God judged Adam because he ate from the tree of the knowledge of good and evil. If Adam hadn't eaten from the tree, he wouldn't have been judged. When Eve turns to give the fruit to Adam, he could have said, "No." If one spouse finds out that the other one is having an affair, that spouse could easily say, "No, I would not stoop that low and sin against my God, body, and mate."
Two wrongs don't make a right, but I guess to some people it makes it even.

God did not allow Adam and Eve to get a divorce. God could have easily made another woman for Adam and another man for Eve. But he didn't. Adam and Eve could have easily gone their separate ways. But they didn't. This story should tell you a lot about God and marriage: "Don't let a snake come between your marriage."

In a marriage, your family is your first responsibility. This not only means their physical needs, but their personal needs, too. There are couples that get caught up in taking care of outsiders but forget to take care of their partner in life.

Divorce is the wrong path, and I wrote this book to help couples get back on the right path. If you're a couple that's thinking about a divorce—don't! Make a commitment to work through your marriage by using this book for one month. If you have put time, effort, and energy toward a divorce, redirect it to repairing your marriage. If your marriage is good, use this book to keep working on it to make it better. This book provides you with valuable insight and guidance about how to make your marriage successful, so that it pleases God and sets a positive example for society.

Table of Content

Preface .... *I*

Introduction .... *III*

Week One: What Is Marriage?

Day 1: There are no bad marriages—only bad couples. 1

Day 2: Marriage is a balance of power between the husband and the wife. 6

Day 3: You can't be single when you're married 11

Day 4: Marriage takes mind, soul, and body. 15

Day 5: Marriage isn't knowing everything about your mate; it's learning about him or her. 20

Day 6: What have you learned from week one? Weekend (Sat.) 24

Day 7: What have you learned from week one? Weekend (Sun.)..25

Week Two: You and Your Mate as a Couple.

Day 8: Accept yourself and your mate for who you both are. 26

Day 9: Who's right or wrong. 30

Day 10: You must have a forgiving and forgetful heart. 34

Day 11: Two lives becoming one. 41

Day 12: Insecurities. 45

Game Day Weekend.

Day 13: Lovemaking and Baseball (Sat.) 49

Day 14: Marriage and Football (Sun.) 55

Week Three: The Marriage.

Day 15: Love. 59

Day 16: The children. 63

Day 17: Money as children. 67

Day 18: Family and Friends..72

Day 19: Marriages keep growing and moving. 77

Weekend: The Four Seasons of Marriage.

Day 20: Time and Communication (Sat.) 81

Day 21: Understanding and Maturity (Sun.) 87

Week Four: 'Til Death Do Us Part.

Day 22: Trust. 91

Day 23: Personal Appearances. 95

Day 24: Time and Space to Self. 99

Day 25: Be a Creative Couple. 103

Day 26: The ten commandments of marriages. 107

Day 27: Evaluate your marriage. 112

Day 28: Marriage Is Chess Not Checkers. 116

Day 29: Can I do all these things? 120

Day 30: Where is God in my marriage? 124

Day 31: Entertainment. 127

Conclusion 131

Week One: What Is Marriage?

Day 1: There are no bad marriages—only bad couples.

Then God saw everything that he had made, and indeed it was very good. So the evening and the morning were the sixth day (Genesis 1:31).

Man was not made for marriage; marriage was made for man. It's a uniquely human institution. It's not a coincidence that the most intelligent beings on earth are the only ones that can choose to be married. There is no other form of life that can experience the joy and commitment of being married. To be married is a breathtaking experience for the man and the woman he desires. Two separate lives combine to be one: This has to be the most beautiful combination in nature. So know this: marriage is special.

Marriage is not just a promise to the other person—it's a promise to humanity and God. This is why there is always a witness to every marriage. The witness can testify that this couple has made a covenant with God and each other. To break these vows is to break the will of God and the cycle of

Day 1: There are no bad marriages-only bad couples.

humanity. Think of what the world would be like if there were no marriages. In a word—chaos. There would be no trust, obligation, family values, or societal structure and order. Who would like to live in a world like that? Marriage brings stability and assurance to a civilized society. Marriage is one of the most important decisions that you will make in your life.

The first is making Jesus your Lord and Savior. The second is whom you will marry. Every marriage must be based in God the Father. There is a higher power in your marriage. Every person needs to be under the authority of someone. There are no loose cannons! We all need to submit. God must be the one we submit to because man is flawed and biased. The husband is the head of the household, and God is the head of him.

What makes marriages bad?

People. When a couple has disagreements each spouse's first thought is to blame the marriage. The marriage is an agreement with God and society. Marriage comes from God, and everything God does is good. Is the problem the agreement? No, the problem is two people who have issues with one another. So instead of saying there is a marriage problem, it should be more accurately described as a couple's problem.

Someone once said, "If you get wet in a rainstorm, don't blame the rain for not having an umbrella." Just as it may be easy to blame the rain when you should be

Day 1: There are no bad marriages-only bad couples.

blaming yourself, we often blame our spouses without admitting our own faults. In a marriage, both spouses need to take a look at how he or she has contributed to the problem. The ability to solve problems is a skill that successful and respected couples have learned over time. Every marriage has bumps in the road. When spouses blame each other, their bumps grow into obstacles that may eventually turn into roadblocks. If you fail to obey a roadblock, you could be killed. If you fail to obey a roadblock in marriage, the result can be death to the marriage—otherwise known as divorce.

Playing the blame game is easier than owning up to your own faults. We can't control our mate, but we can control ourselves. Hopefully and prayerfully our partner will be influenced by our growth in this vital area.

Day 1: There are no bad marriages-only bad couples.

Tips for Day 1
1. Marriage is a gift from God to man.
2. Marriages are a commitment before God and society.
3. Marriage is forever.
4. Marriage is an important step in your life.
5. Couples should evaluate each other.

Your Tips for the Day

Day 1: There are no bad marriages-only bad couples.
Notes for your marriage

Day 2: Marriage is a balance of power between the husband and the wife.

So God created man in his own image; in the image of God he created him; male and female he created them (Genesis 1:27).

Scripture tells us that men and women are created equal. But for centuries men have dominated women. Even in our culture, this is probably the greatest misunderstanding about marriage (especially for men). Some men think that simply because they are the man, their job is to dominate their wife. God gave man dominion over the earth but not his wife. Man is the head of the house, not the dictator of the house. The dictator is always God.

The first thing a husband must do is look at his wife as his equal. He's in charge only because God ordained it that way. A man is not better than a woman but rather equal to her. So when a man looks at his wife, he should see a creature made in the image of God just as he was. Being created in the image of God does not mean men and women are the same. Husbands and wives have different personalities, attitudes, and emotions, to name a few things. A wife can't do everything that her husband can. Likewise there are things that she can do that he can't. (To save myself from embarrassment as a man, I won't get into a numbers game to see who can do the most.) She may be at home, cook food, and watch the kids, but there is more that she can do. Husbands, remember your wives had successful lives before they met you. So men, when it comes to some major decision making, it's best to talk it over with your wife for balance.

Day 2: Marriage is a balance of power between the husband and the wife.

This does not make you less of a man; it makes you more of a man. A balanced marriage makes a balanced home. There are problems in some households because one person directs the house. The sharing of the house should involve the same give and take as sharing love does. Make no mistake about it—the man is the ruler of the house. But for every king, there is a queen, and she has good ideas, too. This helps balance the decision-making power in your marriage. Both spouses need to talk through decisions. If they don't, then it gets into a power contest that no one wins. Learn to use each other's gift as an opportunity to grow together in marriage.

The gift of LOVE: That a man and woman can come together and live at peace with one another. Two minds are always better than one. A man who throws his weight around the house is simply showing his immaturity. A woman who nags all the time is a pain in the you know what. Neither of these actions helps the marriage. A strong wife stands beside her husband because she respects him as her partner. A strong husband is with his wife because he values her as a tremendous woman. The two must come together and make peace in the house. Home time should be the most comfortable time there is. Husbands, the next time you see your wife doing laundry, don't think you are looking at a maid. You're looking at a person that could run a Fortune 500 company (running a family household is harder than running a business). She turned down that

Day 2: Marriage is a balance of power between the husband and the wife.

job to wash your dirty socks because she loves you so much. Wives, the next time you look at your husband remember this: Here is a man that could have chosen another woman, but he chose you.

Day 2: Marriage is a balance of power between the husband and the wife.

Tips for Day 2

1. As husbands, you must learn to share the balance of power not with one who is inferior to you but with a wife who respects you.
2. Wives, husbands have good taste in picking out things for the house too.
3. Husbands, respecting your wife is the same as respecting your mother. Wives, respecting your husband is the same as respecting your father.
4. Husbands, there is no need to flex your muscle in the house; a good wife knows who's in charge.
5. There must be peace in the home.

Your Tips for the Day

Day 2: Marriage is a balance of power between the husband and the wife.

Notes for your marriage_____

_____
_____
_____
_____
_____
_____
_____
_____
_____
_____
_____
_____
_____
_____
_____
_____
_____
_____
_____
_____
_____
_____
_____
_____
_____
_____
_____
_____
_____

Day 3: You can't be single when you're married.

When I was a child, I spoke as a child, I understood as a child, I thought as a child, but when I became a man, I put away childish things (I Corinthians 13:11).

When a man and woman decide they're going to spend the rest of their lives together, there is a crystal-clear change that needs to take place in their lives. The change is the realization that "you are not single anymore." It's a terrible mistake to be married and still act like you're single.

The single life is over for the both of you and some adjustments need to be made. Your life has taken on a whole new meaning and new challenges. When you were single the whole world revolved around you and your wishes: Being single you could go and do whatever you desired with no curfew and no calling to check in. It was just you and the city lights. Those days are over and never to return. Everything is different now (at least it should be) and joyfully so.

Life is made up of different phases, and each phase brings a change in your life. As the saying goes, "You can't be in two places simultaneously."
The same holds true for holy matrimony—you're either married or not. And if you are married, you need to start acting like it.

If you didn't want to be married, then why did you get married? When you committed to being married, you announced to God and the world that your single life was over. So if nothing has changed in the way you act and

Day 3: You can't be single when you're married.

live, you need to ask yourself, "Why not?" Do you argue with your mate using questions like:

"Why can't I go out?"

"Why can't I hang out with my friends?"

"Why can't I live my life as before?"

There is no need to argue and fight with your partner about these questions. These questions show that you don't understand the nature of marriage. If your mate has a problem with you going out, then guess what? Sayonara to the nightlife.

Your life now involves another person, and it's not all about what you want to do. Did you not get the memo? Marriage is honor, love, and respect.

Honor your mate.

Love your mate.

Respect your mate.

You and your spouse may not be on the same page, but at least be in the same book (marriage).

Day 3: You can't be single when you're married.

Tips for Day 3
1. The single life is over and never to return.
2. The most selfish thing you can do in marriage is do what you want to.
3. Having more single friends than married friends should be a red flag. Try to accumulate new friends who enjoy the same lifestyle (a married one).
4. Respecting your mate is respecting your marriage.
5. The single life is hard, and marriage is easy because you only have one person to please.

Your Tips for the Day

Day 3: You can't be single when you're married.

Notes for your marriage_____

_____
_____
_____
_____
_____
_____
_____
_____
_____
_____
_____
_____
_____
_____
_____
_____
_____
_____
_____
_____
_____
_____
_____
_____
_____
_____
_____
_____
_____
_____

Day 4: Marriage takes mind, soul, and body.

And you shall love the Lord your God with all your heart, with all your soul, with all your mind, and with all your strength.' This is the first commandment (Mark 12:30).

When you get married your mind, body, and soul should be one. However, in some marriages the body is the only part that ties the knot.

The Mind

The human mind is the place where thoughts are kept. So, if your mind is married, then your thoughts must be married, too. You cannot have a successful marriage with a single-person's thought life. In order to control your mind, you must control your thoughts. It's impossible for you to have a mind that is focused on being disciplined toward your marriage when your thinking isn't as well.

The Body

"What's mine is yours, and what's yours is mine" does not just pertain to sex. There are other reasons why one spouse would want the other spouses body. For instance, the wife would like to go shopping, and she wants the husband to go. Since your two bodies are now one, I guess we will see you at the mall or maybe she wants you to go to a function with her (although it's game night for you). You need to let the game go, husband, because your wife needs you. Remember, if you don't go, you lose points. One night for a game may cost you

Day 4: Marriage takes mind, soul, and body.

several nights with your wife. Husbands it's the same with you. If you have to go somewhere and desire your wife by your side, then she needs to go. Husbands like their wives to look sexy for them. So, ladies if he picks out your outfit, wear it. Even if it is that time of the month and you don't feel sexy; the outfit is for him, not for you.

The Soul

This is the most intimate part of a person. If you want to get things right, you really need to be at peace here. The soul is the spiritual bridge of the marriage. This is the most important part of a marriage, the soul of your spouse. The problem is that the outside of a person doesn't always tell you what they feel inside.

Have you ever been miserable and depressed and no one knew how you felt, not even your spouse? A person's body can show one way of feeling, but inside he or she is feeling totally different. This is not good for the other mate because he or she has no clue about what is going on. The wife or husband could be in a state of depression, and the other mate doesn't have an inkling that something is wrong. One spouse could be thinking of divorce, and the other doesn't have any indication. One spouse could be mentally disturbed or close to a nervous breakdown because of the stress of the marriage, and the other doesn't have any idea. Why don't both mates know what is happening in their marriage? No one just jumps off a cliff; it takes time to drive up the mountain, get out of the car, and walk to the spot to jump. The question is, where is the other mate and why hasn't he or she seen the signs? Maybe that spouse was too busy getting in touch

<u>Day 4: Marriage takes mind, soul, and body.</u>

with his or her soul (inner peace) than thinking about his or her spouse's soul (inner peace). Learn to put your mate's inner peace before your own; this will give you inner peace. This is a true partnership.

There are always signs before a major crisis that could be easily missed. A spouse did not get like this overnight. It takes time for hurt and pain to build up in a person's heart. The most painful thing for someone is that his or her spouse, person who sleeps next to him or her every night, doesn't know that something is wrong. The only way to know what is in the soul of a person is to ask that person or look for telltale signs.

Sometimes couples tend to look at things from one side of the equation. If your mate tells you that something you did offended him or her, but you felt like you didn't do anything wrong, you still need to apologize to your spouse. If your mate says that you offended him or her (even though you did not mean to), you need to apologize and commit to not doing that again. The problem is that some mates would rather argue than apologize. As a married couple you must be able to know what your soul mate is feeling beyond his or her smile.

<u>Day 4: Marriage takes mind, soul, and body.</u>

Tips for Day 4
1. Don't just think of your inner peace.
2. The husband and wife must be at one in all three aspects (body, soul and mind).
3. Identifying the soul of a person can't always be done by observing his or her behavior.
4. For your mate to tell you what's in his or her soul, he or she must trust you.
5. You have a partner for life.

Your Tips for the Day

Day 4: Marriage takes mind, soul, and body.
Notes for your marriage

Day 5: Marriage isn't knowing everything about your mate; it's learning about him or her.

But the Lord said to Samuel, "Do not look at his appearance or at his physical stature, because I have refused him. For the Lord does not see as man sees; for man looks at the outward appearance, but the Lord looks at the heart" (I Samuel 16:7).

Most immature couples go through this problem of thinking they know their mate. Let me ask you a question: Have you ever done anything that you said that you would never do? If the answer is yes, then you don't know yourself as well as you think you do. So how can you go into a marriage thinking that you know all about the other person when you barely know yourself)?

In marriage you're learning the other person and yourself. Neither person has ever been married to the other, so this marriage is a learning process for the both of you. Each spouse must learn about the other and apply what has been learned to the marriage.

Every marriage should be moving forward and not backward. A married couple should not be arguing about things that happened years ago. The husband and the wife should have some sort of communication about current struggles and not past transgressions. If a couple has been married for two years, then they should have two years' worth of experience in what to do and what not to do. Don't be a broken record arguing and fussing about the same thing. Just as you are learning to deal with your partner, your partner is learning to deal with you. The

<u>Day 5: Marriage isn't knowing everything about your mate; it's learning about him or her.</u>

best thing is to be patient, kind, and respectful to one another. Look at the good things that you have in common. The bad will always be there, but it's your choice to focus on the good. The good will always outweigh the bad if you like to be happy.

    Marriage does not make you happy; hard work in marriage makes you happy. There will be things that you find out about your mate that you didn't know. Don't panic; your mate is also finding out things about you. Everything can be conquered with love and understanding. You would never meet a person with whom you are 100 percent compatible. Don't be deceived—that person doesn't exist. Everybody has his or her view in life and nature. A couple's view might not line up, but the love they share covers the gaps. It's okay if you feel like your spouse has changed since the marriage because you have changed, too. Very few people have received the same type of person they first married (few people remain the same over time). When a couple gets married they will evidently change. The more the two of you are around each other, the more compatible you will become. Keep this in mind: the longer the years in marriage, the more you will learn in marriage about yourself and your mate.

Day 5: Marriage isn't knowing everything about your mate; it's learning about him or her.

Tips for Day 5
1. Your mate will change in the marriage and so will you.
2. You will learn new things about your mate over the years, and he or she will learn new things about you.
3. When you learn something new about your mate don't panic. Your mate has learned something new about you, too.
4. When you finding something out about your mate that you don't like, focus on the things that you do like about your mate.
5. Have patience and understanding when new things occur.

Your Tips for the Day

Day 5: Marriage isn't knowing everything about your mate; it's learning about him or her.

Notes for your marriage

Day 6: What have you learned from week one?
Weekend (Sat.)
Notes for your
marriage_____

Day 7: What have you learned from week one?
Weekend (Sun.)
Notes for your marriage_____

Week Two: You and Your Mate as a Couple.

Day 8: Accept yourself and your mate for who you both are.

"'You shall love your neighbor as yourself.' There is no other commandment greater than these" (Mark 12:31).

Having your partner in a marriage means accepting who you and they are in the big scheme of life (you must accept both yourself and your partner as you both are). There are many husbands and wives that can't get along because they don't live in a realistic world. I have counseled husbands who thought they should have been famous musicians or professional athletes. I have counseled wives who think they should have married a millionaire. In those cases I immediately ask, "Why do you think this way?" Some wives think that they have the body and the looks of a model and that a million-dollar man would love to be with them. There is no way they should be married to Joe the plumber. Some husbands think they can play sports really well or sing and write pretty good songs. There is no way they should be married to Susan the secretary. That's a good thing that they think highly of themselves, but this is overdoing it. The reality of the situation is that you are who you are. If

Day 8: Accept yourself and your mate for who you both are.

you were supposed to be married to Denzel Washington, then you would have married him. If you were such a good rapper, you would have a music contract. Well, guess what aspiring rapper: "Drop the mike and go home to your family!" Be who you are and love who you are married to. Maybe the reason your marriage is not working is because you're trying to be somebody that you're not. If you dress and get a haircut like Brad Pitt, that doesn't mean you're Brad Pitt. If you dress and style yourself like Beyonce, that doesn't mean you deserve her lifestyle. The best marriages are couples that can be themselves. The freedom of marriage is the freedom of being free.

To try to dress and act like someone else puts too much pressure on the marriage. I do understand you have dreams, and you keep fighting to achieve them. But, if your dream is affecting your family life, it's time to "drop the mike and go home." You're married, and now is the time to grow up. Wives, stop spending money trying to look like a Hollywood star; everybody knows you shop at the flea market. "Drop the mike." Stop imagining and fantasizing, and start working on your marriage. Some of your dreams are like birds in a cage; they would fly away, but you keep holding on to them. It's time to get some concrete ideas and "let the birds fly." Married couples love yourself for who you are, not for who you think you should be.

<u>Day 8: Accept yourself and your mate for who you both are.</u>

Tips for Day 8
1. God made you a special person not another person.
2. Everyone is special in his or her own little way.
3. Marriage doesn't mean that your dream is over, but it may have to take a backseat.
4. "Drop the mike" (the *mike* could be any dream that is not coming to pass).
5. You must learn to accept yourself before you can truly accept your mate.

Your Tips for the Day

<u>Day 8: Accept yourself and your mate for who you both are.</u>
Notes for your marriage___

Day 9: Who's right or wrong.

Finally, brethren, whatever things are true, whatever things are noble, whatever things are just, whatever things are pure, whatever things are lovely, whatever things are of good report, if there is any virtue and if there is anything praiseworthy—meditate on these things (Phillippians 4:8).

If a couple argues long enough about the same thing, you would see the conversation eventually change. What started the confrontation is no longer being discussed. The battle now is about who's right and who's wrong. One reason some couples never settle their disagreement is because both want to be right! Even when knowing they're wrong, they have to have the last word.

It's a battle of pride and whose opinion is right. There is more between the lines of right and wrong, just as there are shades of gray in between black and white. Sometimes the best results are when you mix them together. You were right yesterday, so let your spouse be right today. It's all about compromising with your spouse while both of you are learning to live and work together. From my experience, I have come to the conclusion that both parties can be right and wrong.

Look at a half glass of water. The wife may say, "It's half empty." The husband may say, "It's half full." Both are right because the glass of water is half empty and half full. It's not about who's right or wrong. It's about your personal perception of the situation. So the next time you argue with your mate, think about what the problem is

Day 9: Who's right or wrong.

and see if there are other ways to solve it because you both can be right. The disagreement may not be what's being argued about. It may be in the mind of the other person. You can't change that person's mind by fussing and fighting, but you can by understanding his or her point of view.

The best way to solve a disagreement with a person is to look at it from his or her perspective. When you decide to listen to your partner without yelling, it will keep your partner from yelling. You controlled the volume of the conversation and keep your hand on the right button. If you need your mate to quiet down, just turn the volume down. When you are watching TV, and it's too loud, you point the remote and turn it down. The same idea would apply to your mate. You don't yell at the TV to turn it down, push the right buttons. You have your spouse's buttons in your hands; he or she may be yelling and mad because you're pushing the wrong ones!

It's always better to hear people in a settled quiet voice than surround sound. Leave the surround sound for the movies. When you let your partner take control, your emotions and feelings are under his or her control. Don't let your partner get the best of you. Remember, you're talking to solve the problem; yelling and fussing only makes it worse and adds new problems.

<u>Day 9: Who's right or wrong.</u>

Tips for Day 9
1. When having a disagreement with your mate, stick to the conversation.
2. Don't try to figure out who's right or wrong.
3. Some arguments are just different points of view.
4. Your mate maybe making negative comments because you're making negative comments.
5. Every conversation is under your control, not your mate (so push the right buttons).

Your Tips for the Day

Day 9: Who's right or wrong.
Notes for your marriage

Day 10: You must have a forgiving and forgetful heart.

"For if you forgive men their trespasses, your heavenly Father will also forgive you (Matthew 6:14).

There is no crime or act that can't be forgiven, and there is no forgiveness that can't be forgotten. Notice I didn't say forgiving and forgetting wouldn't cause you hurt, pain, and sleepless nights. But this is something that we all must do. Divorce is something that we opt to do while forgiving and forgetting is something that we must do.

Domestic violence in a marriage

Marriage can bring out the best and the worst in people: When it's good, it's good, and when it's bad, it's real bad. Domestic violence is the worst of all crimes against marriages. This is one of the ugliest and most embarrassing situations in a marriage. This type of behavior is irresponsible and can get someone hurt or killed. There are thousands of wives who are in abusive relationships and feel trapped. They don't know what to do or who to talk to. They have many questions and no answers. With a doctorate in theology and as a born again believer, I feel most qualified to answer their questions. "What should I do if my husband is hitting me, but he is not having an extramarital affair?"

I would answer your question:
"I have no commandment of the Lord: yet I give my judgment, as one that hath obtained mercy of the Lord to be faithful" (I Corinthians 7:25). *"But to the rest I, not the Lord speak"* (I Corinthians 7:12)

Day 10: You must have a forgiving and forgetful heart.

What should you do if your husband hits you?
1. Nothing.
2. Don't fight back.
3. Wait until it's safe and call 911.
4. Flee from that man because he's a burning building, a death trap.
5. Tell your mate (when the police arrive), you forgive him, but you're still pressing charges.
6. If for whatever reason you get back together and his court day comes up, you still testify against him.
7. When he goes to jail, tell him you will pray for him and hope no one in there hits him.

No man should hit a woman, and no woman needs a man that hits her (not even once). And no woman should hit a man. If you let that turkey slide with one "snap," he would eat you for breakfast, because "crackle" and "pop" are following. When a husband hits his wife, he's an unbalanced man and can't be trusted. If he thinks he can hit you, then he thinks he can cheat on you. Some wives are staying there trying to keep their marriage, but in reality staying there is destroying it. It's gone from a marriage to an unholy boxing ring, and that's one ring you can't put on your finger. This goes for verbal abuse as well.

Wives stop trying to provoke your husband because you can't beat him in a fight. A man doesn't need to hit a woman, but men don't need a woman that provokes violence. I think one of the most important things in a marriage is for a wife to know when to stop fussing. Ladies have more tolerance in a marriage than men. Men are sometimes on a short fuse, especially when

Day 10: You must have a forgiving and forgetful heart.

there are money problems in the marriage. But with that said, that still isn't an excuse to be hit.

Why?

Because some wives remind the husband every day about how little money they have. When the money's not right, there's pressure on the man. The woman has pressure too, but everything always falls on the man. So wives learn not to tempt your husband: He's already under pressure.

Learn to love him and respect him as a man; even when there isn't enough money to get your cell phone turned back on.

Sometimes the hardest thing to do is the easiest thing to do—like forgiving and forgetting. Someone once asked me, "How can I forgive and forget what my spouse did to me?" Most people think that forgiving and forgetting is all about the person who committed the offense. It's not that simple. Let's look at the situation like a pie. We could divide it up like this: Ten percent is the act, what he or she did to you: Cheated on you, left you, misused you, etc. Another ten percent is the damage (the result of what he or she did). This is the hurt and pain it's caused you. This is the part with which most couples have problems. These two things you can't change, and this adds up to 20 percent. There is no way of changing the past; you must come to the conclusion that what is done is done. This is a small percentage, because you can't spend too much of your time on something you can't change. If your mate lied to you, don't let this thought dominate your mind the whole day. It's of no value or use to you, give it 20 percent and keep moving. The ball is now in

Day 10: You must have a forgiving and forgetful heart.

your court. Your mate lied to you, and you told him or her you forgive him or her...but... Watch out for those buts. Thoughts start going through your mind about what? Why? How? When? And Who? There are too many unanswered questions lingering in your head. The more thoughts that come in your head, the harder it is to find forgiveness.

Why is forgiving so hard?

Because you thought about the offense the whole day, and you have added and taken out things from the story. You think, "Why should I believe his or her story anyway? He or she has already confessed to being a liar." He or she did not confess to being a liar; the confession was that he or she *lied*. Do see the difference here. A liar and a person who told a lie are two different people. If that's not the case, then you could say that one drink makes a person an alcoholic.

Eighty percent of your forgiving and forgetting somebody is for you. Forty percent goes to you **forgetting** about what the person did. In order to help you forgive, first try forgetting what the person did. Work on forgetting first, and then you will forgive automatically. Forty percent of you **forgiving** goes to your mental health and well-being. An unforgiving heart can kill you fast or slow like cancer. In order for you to sustain yourself and your sanity, forgive your mate and move on with the marriage. You say, "I will forgive, but I won't forget." Well, this is not forgiving your mate because every time something occurs, you bring up the same old problems.

Day 10: You must have a forgiving and forgetful heart.

How do you forget about things?

Easy—don't think about them. There're a million and one things that you can think about. Hear my advice. If your mate does something to you that causes you to hurt, take a break for a couple of hours and cry your head off. I am talking about "Middle Eastern" crying—rolling on the floor and throwing dirt from the carpet up in the air. Listen to and sing every sad song that you can think of. Once that is over, get up, wash your face, and go back to work. Because here is a secret: Life moves on! The world can't and won't stop because your spouse offended you no matter how deeply.

Day 10: You must have a forgiving and forgetful heart.

Tips for Day 10
1. Forgiving and forgetting are mandatory.
2. Try forgetting first and then forgiving
3. Marriage is not physical (absolutely no hitting!) or mental abuse.
4. Marriages move on.
5. We all make mistakes.

Your Tips for the Day

Day 10: You must have a forgiving and forgetful heart.
Notes for your marriage

Day 11: Two lives becoming one.

Therefore a man shall leave his father and mother and be joined to his wife, and they shall become one flesh (Genesis 2:24).

The beauty of marriage is when two people come together as one. The wife is the husband's better half while the husband is the wife's better half. The two become one but are still two. So in a marriage you're still dealing with two individuals. It's not wise or beneficial to counsel just one mate because there are two sides to every story. This is the situation that some in-laws get into. They only hear and believe one side of the story. This is not fair to the other person.

Marriage takes work from both sides, not just one. If one mate has an issue, then the other is involved as well. Let's say that the wife is at home sick with the flu. If the husband is not working or doing something for the family, he should be at home with his wife. It doesn't look too pretty, if the wife is sick, and the husband is at the club. I am not suggesting the husband catch the flu because his wife is sick. What I mean is the husband should be there taking care of his better half. A man and woman become married—peanut butter and jelly become a sandwich.

These two things just go together and make the situation better and taste good. When couples are away from each other something should be missing. You should have a strong desire to be with your loved one. If you don't have these feeling, then you need to do some checks and balances on your marriage. A man can't live

<u>Day 11: Two lives becoming one.</u>

too long without his rib. GET EXCITED ABOUT YOUR MATE. GET EXCITED ABOUT LIFE!

There are many people in the world that wish they had somebody to love; somebody to care for them regardless of their faults. In a marriage, no spouse is perfect, but together both become perfection. What a masterpiece to see two people together in harmony. Life is good when you're living it like this.

<u>Day 11: Two lives becoming one.</u>

Tips for Day 11
1. Marriage is two people with one purpose (happiness).
2. There're two sides to every story, so don't be so quick to take sides.
3. Husbands and wives go together like peanut butter and jelly (it makes a good sandwich).
4. Enjoy your family.
5. There are people who wish they were happily married.

Your Tips for the Day

<u>Day 11: Two lives becoming one.</u>
Notes for your marriage_____

Day 12: Insecurities.

Therefore, if anyone is in Christ, he is a new creation; old things have passed away; behold, all things have become new (II Corinthians 5:17).

Most of the time this is something that bothers the wife, but there are husbands who feel the same way, too. There are two main reasons why someone may feel insecure:
1. He or she was brought up with feelings of insecurity.
2. He or she has become insecure because of the things his or her spouse had said in past arguments.

This is a good reason why married couples shouldn't argue. When people get mad anything will fly out of their mouths. When the arguing session is long over, those words you said are still floating around in the air. Sometimes these words find their way into your mate's spirit (heart and mind).

Your words and your actions can make your spouse feel insecure. Every couple must be careful with the words they choose to say to their life partner. One person may not be as strong as the other, therefore, your words should be chosen very carefully. Bad words (i.e., insults, taunts, or profanity) only tear down a marriage, and most of the time, you can't take them back. If you feel like you are starting to get angry: STOP ARGUING! Walk away. Don't say anything or you may be sorry later.

If your mate feels insecure, you can help him or her feel more secure. Building up your mate is one of the most

<u>Day 12: Insecurities.</u>

important things you can learn. You help your mate feel secure by doing and saying the right things. Follow these examples to raise your mate's self esteem:
- Complementing him or her on how good he or she looks.
- Asking if there is anything that you can do for him or her.
- Letting him or her know that marrying him or her was the best decision you have ever made.
- Tell him or her how much you appreciate him or her and all the things he or she does.
- Tell him or her that you don't know what you would do without them.

These words go far and deep.

Day 12: Insecurities.

Tips for Day Twelve
1. Stop arguing.
2. Your words can build or tear down your marriage.
3. You can attract more bees with honey.
4. Make your mate feel secure.
5. Hold tight to your spouse and don't ever let go.

Your Tips for the Day

<u>Day 12: Insecurities.</u>
Notes for your marriage

Game Day Weekend.

Day 13: Lovemaking and Baseball (Sat.)

The wife does not have authority over her own body, but the husband does. And likewise the husband does not have authority over his own body, but the wife does (I Corinthians 7:4).

If you know the game of baseball and use its strategy in lovemaking, then you will please your wife. There are many husbands who wonder: "When it comes to sex, am I pleasing my wife?" Men ask this question because there may be a little insecurity on their part. And I would assume my reader knows what part I'm talking about (being a good lover in bed).

Married men, this is the fact of life: "All men are not created equal." Just think of it like baseball. There're some power hitters and some average hitters. The point is that everyone will get their time at bat with their personal pitcher (their wife). You must be able to work with the bat that nature gave you. When you're about to go to the plate (foreplay), focus on the game (making love). Don't worry and don't ask about who was at bat before you (asking your wife about her sex life before she married you). It's

Day 13: Lovemaking and Baseball (Sat.)

none of your business and has nothing to do with the game that is being played now.

When your wife throws the pitch, your job is to hit the ball. I know this is a serious issue for some players because some wives throw lots of change-up pitches. One mistake you shouldn't make is trying to hit every pitch out the ballpark. There are many other ways you can score. A baseball game is nine innings, so pace yourself. It's the power hitter that has the most strike outs (if you know what I mean).

Guys, when you step up to the plate (the batter's box) you must know your pitcher (wife). Good baseball players always study films on their opponent. Some husbands have been with their wives for three to four years and still don't know how to hit the ball.

Why?

Because they don't study the pitcher. They just go out and swing at any pitch she throws. In the marriage game, the pitcher is not happy when you strike out (that means negative points against you). Husbands know your wives, and wives, know your husbands. In the game of baseball, all eyes are on the hitter and when the wife pitches, and the hitter hits, it's always a good game. Not all balls can be hit. Sometimes there are foul balls and wild pitches (you can discuss these things with your wife). Good hitters look at the pitcher and from knowing her, have a good idea of what type of ball she's about to

Day 13: Lovemaking and Baseball (Sat.)

throw. Don't let the bat tell the ball what to do. Let the ball tell the bat how to hit it (Marriage terms: don't let your thing tell you what to do, let her thing tell you what to do). Back at the batter's box, you seen this position before: "She is about to throw a curve ball." That means you can only take what she gives you, first base. Take the base and be glad that you have a man in scoring position. The difference between baseball and lovemaking is that baseball has nine innings, but the wife decides how many innings are in this game. She may only want one inning tonight, or she may be in the mood for seventeen innings (may the Lord help you). She may pitch you fastballs every inning, or she may see that you are tired and let you walk. The game is hers to play not yours.

For the batter, it's just like professional baseball: you win the game using your mind and your skills. A word to the wise, you can't win every game with your skills alone. The only thing the husband needs to do is stay in the batter's box. Keep the bat in his hand (You drop that bat, and you've just dropped the game). As a man, I understand how difficult it can be to try to stay in the box with pitches being thrown at you, holding on to the bat. We are not robots. We have feelings, too. The pitcher doesn't care. You just better not drop that bat.

If you do, you're going to get talked about real bad. This is what the off-season is all about. We must stay in shape by exercising, working out, eating right, etc. In a baseball game when you see guys run to first base, and they're out of breath, you can guarantee they had a bad

Day 13: Lovemaking and Baseball (Sat.)

off-season. They were not training and are out of shape. Men, stay in shape and work hard during the off-season (your down time).

Size doesn't matter in baseball. The question is "What are your batting percentages?" In baseball there are two ways a player can get points: home runs and run batted in. Usually the big guys are always trying to hit home runs. The pitch doesn't matter; curve ball, slider or whatever, they're swinging, trying to hit the ball out of the park. They feel like every pitch is a potential home run. This is why it's so important to know your wife, so you won't be caught by surprise and can anticipate the speed of her pitch. Then you won't be so insecure about a pinch hitter (other hitter taking your place) coming in to replace you.

Day 13: Lovemaking and Baseball (Sat.)

Tips for Day 13
1. Good lovemaking is more mental than physical.
2. Men, be happy with your asset and work with it.
3. If you know more about baseball than your wife, "shame on you."
4. Talk to your wife about lovemaking.
5. "Don't drop that bat!"

Your Tips for the Day

Day 13: Lovemaking and Baseball (Sat.)
Notes for your marriage

Day 14: Marriage and Football (Sun.)

Let the husband render to his wife the affection due her, and likewise also the wife to her husband (I Corinthians 7:3).

The object of any game played is to win and the team with the most points wins. This is the same idea for marriage. The more points you earn, the better chance you have of winning in your marriage.

Let's look at a football team. You have two sets of players that make up the team: The offense and defense. Throughout the game, one of these two sets of players is on the field. In marriage, it's the same way. You're on the offense (being sweet and kind and earning points) or you're on the defense (defending yourself and trying not to lose points). You are not playing against your wife; you are playing with her. When you get married you're playing for happiness, peace, joy, and so on. Any good coach (husband) will tell you "don't beat yourself by turning the ball over." The coach that wins the football game is the coach that understands the game.

Couples, how can you win in marriage when you don't understand the concept? During the course of a game, lots of things are happening. Sometimes it's first and ten (your wife is smiling at you while she's cooking your dinner) and sometimes it's fourth and twenty (you ticked her off because you took your shoes off in the dining room while she was cooking). Whether it's first and ten or fourth and twenty, the coach (husband) calls the plays.   **Let's look at a play**

To win the game you must score points by touchdowns or field goals. Do you understand that,

Day 14: Marriage and Football (Sun.)

coach? Try to score every time you get the ball because in this game you'll never know when you're going to get the ball again (the ball is her smile). Not only do you score points to win, you must stop the other team from scoring points. What good is it if you score every time you get the ball, and then allow the other team to score every time they get the ball?

Example

Your wife asks you to go by the store on your way home from work, but you forgot. The defense (you) just allowed a score. You can't believe she is upset for the rest of the night. The score is seven to zero, and you're losing. The next day, while she's at work, you send her flowers. The offense just scored, but it's only a field goal, and you're still down three to seven. In a marriage you don't do something wrong and then something right, and think everything is okay.

Football talk: You don't score on the offense and turn around and let the defense score.

Let's look at it this way: Suppose you did stop by the store on your way home. Then the next day at work you sent her flowers. Okay, that's ten points. The score is ten to zero, and you're winning. If you really want more points, do things for her before she asks you.

Now let's look at it another way: On your way home from work you called your wife and asked, "Do you need anything while I'm out?" That's fourteen points easily! Hopefully, you get it. The wife decides the points, and your job is to keep scoring.

Day 14: Marriage and Football (Sun.)

Tips for Day 14

1. The more points you have in marriage the better your chances are of staying married.
2. The more points you have, the more she will smile.
3. Don't make points and give them back. And don't turn the ball over.
4. Be a master of both offense and defense.
5. Understand the game and you will win the game.

Your Tips for the Day

Day 14: Marriage and Football (Sun.)
Notes for your marriage___

Week Three: The Marriage.

Day 15: Love.

With all lowliness and gentleness, with longsuffering, bearing with one another in love (Ephesians 4:2).

This is one of the most powerful words we have in our language today. Love is commanding, yet graceful in its own way. You need love for marriage, but marriage is much more than love. Love is the most beautiful feeling that one could have in his or her heart and when one gets married, love develops and grows. The special thing about love is it affects everyone and everything around you. Love makes you love.

There are different types of love:
>The love you have for God.
>The love you have for a child.
>The love you have for a hobby.
>The love you have for your parents.

These are just a few channels of love, but what about the love you have for your mate? All of these loves come with different feelings and different emotions. Before you can love your mate, you must love yourself. You can't give love if you don't have love for yourself. One beautiful aspect of marriage is how you can love your spouse with all that is in you. I personally show my wife not just love from my pocket, but love from all of my being.

God designed the system so that we can show and give love:

Day 15: Love.

> Spiritually.
> Emotionally.
> Physically.

There are people who get married with love, but they are missing the whole experience of being in love. Couples can fall out of love with each other. The more time you spend with someone doesn't necessarily mean that your love is growing for him or her. You must channel your love toward that person.

Day 15: Love.

Tips for Day 15
1. Love is real.
2. Love must be channeled to your mate.
3. There can be no marriages without love.
4. There must be a show and tell of love in the marriage.
5. Marriage is an expression of love.

Your Tips for the Day

Day 15: Love.
Notes for your marriage_____

Day 16: The children.

Train up a child in the way he should go, and when he is old he will not depart from it (Proverbs 22:6).

The children play a big role in a marriage. There must be an understanding of both parents about the way they will raise their children. One spouse shouldn't override the other's authority especially in front of the children. There are two rules I would like to go over in this chapter.
Rule One:
There can't be any arguing in front of the children. Whatever differences you and your mate have, the children should not be exposed to it. The children don't need to see their parents arguing, fussing, and fighting. It would do the children a good service to never see their mom and dad quarrel with each other. How can you tell the children not to fight when they see you fighting? Most children mimic what they see and ignore what they are told.
Rule Two:
Children shouldn't ask one parent a question and then ask the other parent the same question, hoping for a different answer. The child may ask the mom to go to a dance, the mom says no. The child then goes to the father and asks him, and he says yes, unaware that his wife said no. When children do this, they are trying to get the parents to disagree with one another. Both parents must agree when it comes to the children. If they come to you and ask you for something, you should ask them,
"Have you asked the other parent?" If they did, you ask them, "What did the other parent say?" To prevent this

Day 16: The children.

from happening, both parents should divide the decision making.

For example

If you have an older girl, the father should be in charge of the dating issues: who she is going out with, where they are going, what time should she return home, etc. Of course, the girl can talk to her mother about a date, but it's up to her dad on the dating rules. Your children's structure should be organized just like your marriage. Mothers, if you like the guy and think she should go out with him, discuss this with the father first, not the child.

Some children are smarter than you think. If they see a rip in the marriage authority, they are going to take advantage of it. Your children could be plotting against you and playing on your weakness in the marriage. You can have problems with your mate, but the children don't have to know.

<u>Day 16: The children.</u>

Tips for Day 16
1. No arguing, fussing and fighting in front of the children.
2. No undermining one another with the children.
3. Talk about how you are going to raise the children.
4. The children are a part of the marriage.
5. Don't underestimate your children.

Your Tips for the Day

Day 16: The children.
Notes for your marriage

Day 17: Money as children.

A feast is made for laughter, and wine makes merry; But money answers everything (Ecclesiastes 10:19).

One of the biggest problems in marriages today is money. Having money in a marriage is very necessary and important. For you to understand the concept of money, I am going to substitute money for a child. Looking at money from this perspective will help you learn to appreciate it more.

I think you need to watch over your money like you do your children. There are some places where you wouldn't let your child play. The same should hold true with your money. There are some places that your money shouldn't be. You don't let your child wander off not knowing where he is. So why do you allow your money to do it? Just like you check on your kids at bedtime, you need to check on your bank account at bedtime (to see what came in and what went out). Think of your money like your children, you wouldn't let anyone kidnap your children; so don't let anyone kidnap your money.

There are predators who are watching our kids and predators that are watching our money. The world system is designed to take your money, and you better get a plan to protect it. People lost money during the recession trying to make money instead of protecting and saving it. As a husband, you are the watchman over the city (your family). A word to the wise: *The more money you spend, the less money you have. The less money you spend, the more money you have.*

Day 17: Money as children.

Every marriage should have a savings account (make a habit of making automatic deposits). This account should be for vacations, emergencies and what not. If all your money is going to paying bills, you're in big trouble. As the husband, you must do something to fix this problem. The first thing you need to do is look around the house and see what expenses you can cut. The husband and the wife should get together, list the bills, and prioritize them. Cut the things you can live without and cut them quick. The husband should go first and start cutting his stuff. Why the husband first? Because he is the head of the house. If there is only room for one cell phone the wife should have it.

    As a couple you must save money and be wise about the money you're spending. One hundred dollars in your bank account with a pair of no-name brand shoes makes you feel good. Zero dollars in your bank account with a pair of brand name shoes makes you broke.

    When you save money and have money in the bank, you feel different about yourself. You can't spend money like you did before you were married. The money you saved says a lot about you. If you don't have money saved then that says a lot about you, too. If you look after your money like you look after your children, then you wouldn't have financial problems. When you look at your children you feel responsible for them because you made them. Well you made your money, too, so why not feel responsible for that? Money doesn't make a marriage work, but it makes it a lot smoother. This goes out to the women who make more than their man. Just because you

Day 17: Money as children.

make more doesn't mean you can spend more. As a woman, your first priority is to mind your family and preserve the marriage savings account—not your handbags and pumps. If you want name-brand stuff, go to a name-brand flea market. As a good wife, your marriage should come first for you. Wives, you must help your husband budget the money. You are there to support and help your husband. Support is needed when you see him having two jobs, and you have none. Help is needed when the electricity is off, and he got new sneakers. If there is a need for more money in the house, the wife can work to help. Sometimes the wife doesn't have to work; she just needs to change her shopping habits. Working together as a couple will help you gain the financial success you both desire for your family.

<u>Day 17: Money as children.</u>

Tips for Day 17
1. Money is important in a marriage.
2. Watch over your money like you watch over your children.
3. Money doesn't grow on trees; it comes from hard work.
4. Wives watch your shopping habits.
5. It takes money to make money, and to make money, you shouldn't spend all your money.

Your Tips for the Day

Day 17: Money as children.
Notes for your marriage

Day 18: Family and Friends.

So they said, "Believe on the Lord Jesus Christ, and you will be saved, you and your household" (Acts 16:31).

Some marital problems that become hard to resolve usually stem from the influence of family and friends. We will start with friends first because these people are optional. The in-laws are part of the relationship, but friends could be a difference of opinion.

Before you married, you had friends that were close to you. You talked to them while you were engaged and invited them to your wedding. It just so happened that some of these friends are of the opposite sex. This may cause a problem in your marriage with your mate. Your better half may feel like you need to let these people go now that you're married. But you're thinking if you introduce these friends to your spouse, he or she might let you keep your friendship with them. Uunnnk! You thought wrong! Your mate doesn't care for them and asked you to break ties with them.

What should you do?

I never tell people what to do in my counseling session. I only give them the facts of the situation. You're married to your mate, not your friends. You have developed friendships with your friends. Now you need to develop one with your mate. So if those friendships are a distraction to your mate, it would be wise to let them go. It doesn't matter if you strongly disagree with your mate. Marriage is two becoming one. If your mate is happy, then you will be happy. If your mate is troubled, then you will be troubled. Two disturbed mates over one little

Day 18: Family and Friends.

single friend, is not a good situation. "Be wise my little grasshopper."

The Family

When two people get married, their family members come along as a side order. You want the chicken but the fries, biscuit, and drink comes with the meal. You can toss the side orders, but it makes more sense to enjoy them as extras. Don't try to separate your mate from his or her family. These are the people who took care of your mate before you came along. And they would probably be there for them when or if something happened to you.

These three rules should help you.
Rule One:
You're not marrying your mate's family; you're marrying *into* the family. His or her family may be totally different from your family. Accept this and move on.
Rule Two:
You can't force your spouse on your family. If he or she doesn't want to go to your mother's house, it's better if he or she doesn't.
Rule Three:
Don't talk bad about your spouse's family. Your spouse may agree with you at that moment, but this could come back to haunt you.

Of course, it will help you as a couple if you can get along with each other's families, but your mate knows his

Day 18: Family and Friends.

or her family better than you. That family might look like this: The mama talks too much, the daddy doesn't look anything like them, little brother or sister talks about ex-friends, and the uncle or aunt stares at your butt when you walk by, making you feel so uncomfortable.

Look at it this way: if you want to know all about your spouse, listen to his or her drunken uncle or aunt at the Thanksgiving dinner. Give them a couple of drinks, and he or she will spill stone cold truths as if confessing his or her own sins! This relative may say all types of things about your mate, but remember he or she is tipsy (have fun with your mate's family). If you can't laugh with them, then laugh at them.

Day 18: Family and Friends.

Tips for Day 18
1. You can ask your mate to drop their friend(s), but his or her not family.
2. We all understand that sometimes friends are more important than family, but your mate is more important than them all.
3. Try your best to get along with your mother-in-law and father- in-law.
4. Let your mate criticize his or her own family.
5. And remember to smile when you go around them. After all, they might not like you either!

Your Tips for the Day

Day 18: Family and Friends.
Notes for your marriage_____

Day 19: Marriages keep growing and moving.

I affirm, by the boasting in you which I have in Christ Jesus our Lord, I die daily (I Corinthians 15:31).

Marriage is a never-ending journey. It causes you to grow and learn about yourself and your mate. All marriages should be growing. The question is, "are the two of you experiencing this wonderful growth individually or together?" You may not be growing at the same pace, but that's okay. The important thing is that you're learning and growing with each other.

When you're growing it should teach you not to make the same mistake twice. It's puzzling to me to see people in marriages keep making the same mistakes. What are they thinking? Why keep making the same mistakes when you know better? You must grow up in your marriage. Doing the same wrongs will never bring the right results. A person's patience can only be tried so much and for so long, until tolerating each other is no longer an option. As a married couple you must keep this from happening by making sure your mate is not at his or her breaking point. If you keep doing the same wrong thing over and over again, you could bring your spouse to a breaking point in your marriage! My wife and I went on a date with a couple that's been married for five years. When dinner was over I was thinking, "They behaved as if it was their second date." The marriage has grown five years, but the couple behaved like they had been together five days! A planned, lovely evening was wasted by two immature people arguing about things that girlfriends

<u>Day 19: Marriages keep growing and moving.</u>

and boyfriends should be arguing about, not married people.

Not only are marriages growing, but they're moving too. If you can't keep up, you're going to be left behind. What this means is, if you been married for a certain amount of years you should have something to show for it (more than clothes). Don't let the marriage pass you by just like you don't let technology pass you by. Don't be up on technology and down on marriage. If you can keep up with the latest and greatest in communication, then you should be able to keep up your marriage and family.

Quiz yourself

First...
Tell me about smart cell phone.
What is the best game on X Box or Play Station?
Is your TV 1080i?

Now...
Tell me about your mate without any curse words.
What is the best time you have shared together?
What is his or her favorite color?

If the first list is three pages and the second list is a paragraph, you are in big trouble!

<u>Day 19: Marriages keep growing and moving.</u>

Tip for Day 19
1. Learn to grow and move with your marriage.
2. Don't put off for tomorrow, what you can do today.
3. Act your age, not your shoe size.
4. If you know more about Play Station, than your mate, there is a problem.
5. Husbands and wives grow together in the marriage.

Your Tips for the Day

Day 19: Marriages keep growing and moving.
Notes for your marriage

Weekend: The Four Seasons of Marriage.

Day 20: Time and Communication (Sat.)

And the tongue is a fire, a world of iniquity. The tongue is so set among our members that it defiles the whole body, and sets on fire the course of nature; and it is set on fire by hell (James 3:6).

Time and communication, these two words are like rhythm and melody in a marriage. If they work apart from each other, they don't sound as good, but used together will give you sweet harmony. These two are very important for *hot-button topics*. (These are issues that a person needs to get off of his or her chest. They're not good news, but with a careful and diligent hand, they can be easily discussed).

Time

Timing is important in a marriage because there is a time for everything. Communication is just as important because there is a place for everything.

Time = Time to Talk
Communication = Place to Talk

<u>Day 20: Time and Communication (Sat.)</u>

There are things that need to be addressed in your marriage, but the time and place should be right. Just because you have something to say doesn't mean you should say it right then. Wait for the right time and place, then deliver your message. For instance, being in the car with your mate, going to church is not the time to ask past questions such as:

"Where were you when I called you last week?"

"Who was that person sitting by you at the basketball game last month?"

Or worse, "What happened at the bachelor party four years ago?"

This is not the time for that conversation. There are people that can hold stuff in, and then there are those who can't hold their peace at all. Often the problem is *where* and *when* you are trying to have the talk.

It's not a good idea to be excited on the way to a concert and get blindsided with a hostile question that requires an explanation. When you are going to a particular place or event the best thing to do is to think about where you're going. Focus on where you are, instead of where you came from. Enjoy your time together. The problems will still be at home when you get back, so there's no reason to bring them with you. Before my wife and I go on vacation I tell her, "I only bought two tickets and booked one hotel room. I didn't bring enough money for problems. Why would I want problems to come when they're the reason I'm leaving? We will see

Day 20: Time and
Communication (Sat.)

them when we get back. No need to bring them. They'll be there when we return."

Communication

Then there is the communication aspect of things: Sometimes the presentation of the message is worse than the message itself. When the time is right, you'll be able to ask your mate something that has been on your mind. The way you ask him or her will be the way he or she will respond. If you raise your voice, then your spouse probably will raise his or hers. As the husband or wife, you should know that you're the only person that can get under your spouse's skin. Don't go into a conversation expecting to argue. When you have hot-button topics, handle them with care because if you don't, you are preparing to step inside of a shouting ring. Know this before you start your conversation: You started the conversation, and you control the conversation. If you end up arguing, it may have been because of your mishandling of the situation. The first thing that will come out of your mouth is "he or she started yelling." Well, with you being his or her spouse, you should know how to talk to him or her without him or her yelling. The goal of this book is to get you to see marriage the way God sees it. You and your mate are two in one. You must know your mate and keep getting to know him or her. When you ask a question, you're the one who sets the tone for the answer.

For instance, wives: Why would you ask your husband a hot-button question when he is watching the game and its fourth and goal with nine seconds left on the

Day 20: Time and
Communication (Sat.)

clock? Don't be surprised and heartbroken when he answers you sounding irritated. (If he answers at all!) You know that he is watching the game, and it's almost over. Have a little patience, talk to him before the game or after. If you don't, your husband may appear rude because of your approach, timing, and poor communication. This isn't right on his part, but waiting patiently is a virtue.

<u>Day 20: Time and
Communication (Sat.)</u>

Tips for Day 20
1. Time plus communication equals time and place.
2. When it's a hot-button topic, check the time and place.
3. When going to special events or on vacations, leave the problems at home.
4. Wives, understand game day; you got all week to talk about hot-button topics.
5. Don't be rude to your mate.

Your Tips for the Day

Day 20: Time and Communication (Sat.)
Notes for your marriage

Day 21: Understanding and Maturity (Sun.)

Wisdom is found on the lips of him who has understanding, But a rod is for the back of him who is devoid of understanding (Proverbs 10:13).

In the previous chapter we discussed appropriate times and places for hot-button topics. Now, we will look at the receiver's part of this conversation. No one likes to hear bad news about himself or herself, especially when it's coming from the one he or she loves.

Understanding and maturity are just as or maybe more important than the concepts of time and place. Time and place are important to save you from being embarrassed or ruining the mood for something; understanding and maturity affect communication and empathy with your mate. This will keep you from sleeping on the couch!

Understanding

When your mate is telling you his or her hot-button topics, you should be all ears. Hearing the words of your loved one should give you more understanding of why and how he or she is feeling this way. You are listening for two purposes and two purposes only: how to apologize and why you should apologize. The *how* is for you and the *why* is for your spouse. Being the recipient of bad news, often times our first thought is to defend ourselves. You're not a lawyer, and this is not a courtroom —yet. So please listen. When listening to your spouse don't try to think of a defensive strategy to get the verdict you want.

Day 21: Understanding and Maturity (Sun.)

Mature

Once you have allowed your mate to tell his or her issues to you, and you have completely understood where he or she is coming from, it is now time for you to be mature about the whole thing. Of course, you don't agree because you're smarter, but we have learned that "it's not about who's right or wrong." The only thing that matters is that you're off the couch and back in the bed. Maturity in a marriage is replaced with peace in a marriage. If you and your mate are mature adults, then your marriage would be mature. If only one spouse is mature or both are immature, then allow me to schedule you an appointment at 9:00 A.M. on Monday because you will need counseling.

Day 21: Understanding and Maturity (Sun.)

Tips for the Day 21

1. Understanding and maturity are important in a marriage.
2. Don't try to put up a defense all the time.
3. You're listening for two purposes: How and why to *apologize*.
4. Having maturity is having peace.
5. If maturity is lacking in your marriage, schedule an appointment with a counselor—you will need it.

Your Tips for the Day

Day 21: Understanding and Maturity (Sun.)
Notes for your marriage

Week Four: 'Til Death Do Us Part.

Day 22: Trust.

The heart of her husband safely trusts her; So he will have no lack of gain. She does him good and not evil all the days of her life (Proverbs 31:11-12).

A marriage without trust has a name: *stress*. If there is a trust problem in the marriage, stress is not too far behind. This is an issue that is shared by the accused and accuser. The problem with most of these accusations is the absence of proof. Naturally people have a tendency to react based on feelings or hunches, but those are not reliable when solving marital problems. My advice to you is do not accuse your mate of something unless there is clear evidence.

If you have caught your mate cheating, then that's another story. They have given you the right to be suspicious and act on your hunches and feelings. But for now, we are going to highlight the innocent bystanders (mates): The people who can't go to the store by themselves without being accused of going to somebody's house. This is not the code to live by. It's not fair to your mate, and it's not fair to the children. When the children have school the next day, and it's not healthy waking them up to go to the store with their daddy to make sure he comes right back. What is wrong with you? Or your wife is sleeping and you decide to go through her purse. She wakes up and asks you, "What are you doing?" Now

Day 22: Trust.

you're lying when you tell her "Just looking for some gum, honey. Go back to sleep." Or, the husband is taking a shower, and the wife is hiding in the closet going through his cell phone. Stop. Please. Just stop!

Why are you trying to find dirt on your mate? Why are you looking for trouble? Will it make you feel better if your mate tells you he or she is cheating on you? Will that help you get a goodnight's sleep? If the answer is no, then stop accusing your mate of something because your stomach is upset (this is where your feelings and hunches are). It's probably gas.

Nobody wants to get his or her heart broken, so stop wasting time looking for problems when there aren't any. If your spouse is cheating, trust me it is going to come out. You don't have to listen to him or her talking in his or her sleep, hoping he or she will mention a name. Again, what is wrong with you? Stop. Grow up—it will only make the relationship healthier in the end.

Day 22: Trust.

Tips for Day 22
1. No one is cheating on you.
2. Stop accusing your mate of cheating.
3. Other than thinking negative of them be positive.
4. Why would they cheat on you anyway?
5. Are you sure they're the one who can't be trusted?

Your Tips for the Day

Day 22: Trust.
Notes for your marriage

Day 23: Personal Appearances.

But you, when you fast, anoint your head and wash your face (Matthew 6:17).

I'm sorry if I might offend anyone, but personal appearance in a marriage is very important. I would hope that everyone would like to always look presentable to his or her spouse. Some married couples are just really comfortable with each other, but there are some that are not. For example, there are some couples that don't mind using the bathroom in front of each other. (If this works for you, then good; keep doing it). To some this may look disgusting, disturbing, and be considered an invasion of privacy, but this is something that makes them feel closer; their version of "wasted time."

Not all people are on the same level, so take no offense if your mate wants to shut the door. (This is probably a good idea anyway.) Your spouse doesn't have to be happy with everything you do. So instead of forever holding your peace, don't hesitate to communicate that you are not comfortable with certain things he or she does.

Mates, you may not be on the single market anymore, but this does not mean you have to wait a month to go to the barbershop or beauty salon. You tied the knot and personal grooming is more important now than ever.

Why?

Because you are with your spouse for the rest of your life, and you don't want to go from being the apple of his or her eye to the butt of his or her jokes. For example, a wife

Day 23: Personal Appearances.

tells her husband, "You look like a bum asking for spare change when you don't shave or cut your hair." The husband replies, "When you don't put on makeup, you look just like your mama (and her mother is eighty! The wife's thirty). These are dangerous jokes!

When you were single, if you had a bad hair day, it was okay. You could just stay out of sight all day. Being married you will never be out of sight (maybe out of mind). If you don't keep yourself up, don't get mad if you go to church or some other event and see some well-groomed person looking at your partner. (That person is looking nice and neat while you look tired and lazy.)

Day 23:Personal Appearances.

Tips for the Day 23
1. Personal appearance is important in a marriage.
2. If you feel good, then look good. If you feel bad that doesn't give you a ticket to look bad.
3. Keep your edge in marriage (your good looks).
4. Looks can be deceiving, but everybody should want to look his or her best.
5. Your spouse married you, so he or she some physical attraction for you.

Your Tips for the Day

Day 23: Personal Appearances.
Notes for your marriage___

Day 24: Time and Space to Self.

And when He had sent the multitudes away, He went up on the mountain by Himself to pray. Now when evening came, He was alone there (Matthew 14:23).

Each person in a marriage needs his or her own private time and space. This is very healthy and helpful for the marriage. Just like when you were single and didn't feel like going anywhere, and you stayed home, read a book, or watched a movie. Well in marriage, you still need that same time to yourself. You figure "I can't do that anymore because I'm married." This is not true. When you were single you occasionally took a break from the nightlife. You did it not because you were single but human. All humans need a break—a time to think and do nothing, and a time to relax and get refreshed. Even animals wander off from the pack and then come back to the group.

At work you are a target for stress whether it's a high or low and that is why you get breaks. It's unfortunate, but you have to return because you have a mortgage to pay.

Speaking of mortgages, it's even more important to get away from the house when the children are a handful, the husband or wife is annoying, or even the pets are too much of a hassle. You are definitely going to need more than fifteen minutes to make sure you don't plead insanity!

Time to self is for the better, but it has limits. This time doesn't mean a trip to Las Vegas without your spouse. (We've seen the commercial: "What happens in Vegas, stays in Vegas.") This is not the type of time to self

Day 24: Time and Space to Self.

I'm mean. I am not going to give you a pass to destroy your marriage because you want to party.

Time to self could be a weekend to go fishing or camping while the wife goes to the spa. Even if you don't have the opportunity to go out of town, a walk in the park will suffice. This will give you time to breath and enjoy the fresh air of life. This moment of silence and divine peace is awarded just for you.

Sometime marriages are going so fast that you forget the freshness of life and nature. Enjoy your time to yourself and don't abuse it.

Day 24: Time and Space to Self.

Tips for Day 24
1. Each spouse needs to make time for himself or herself.
2. It's good for the health and wealth of the marriage.
3. It could be a walk in the park.
4. This is relaxing and refreshing.
5. Don't abuse this time; use it wisely.

Your Tips for the Day

Day 24: Time and Space to Self.
Notes for your marriage

Day 25: Be a Creative Couple.

Let your fountain be blessed, And rejoice with the wife of your youth (Proverbs 5:18).

This is a strange mystery in some marriages. How can two people who were the life of the party when they were single, get married, and suddenly become the walking dead? This is very puzzling to me that some couples are just flat out boring. Marriage is not the end of life; it is the beginning of a new and better life. You could ask some couples "What did you do exciting last month? Wait for the answer. What's taking them so long to answer? Are they scratching their heads? Do they look nervous? Are they looking around? They must be about to lie.

Marriage is not boring; people who lack a sense of adventure and spontaneity are merely boring. When you were single it was "living for the weekend!" Now that you're married it's "thank God I made it through another week! No wonder some people look excited when they're getting a divorce; they're just dying to live again. You should make it hard for your spouse to leave you! No matter what you do or how frequently you make mistakes (there are limits) divorce should become a foreign word to both of you. You should make it so difficult for your mate to leave you that they would rather walk through fire wearing gasoline drenched underwear than leave you. The only way to get your spouse to that point is to be creative. Creativity comes from within. You shouldn't have to buy your way into having an imagination.

Day 25: Be a Creative Couple.

Example:

For the husband: Music is the key to unlocking the soul. Find out your mate's favorite song or type of music. This is where your creativity comes in to play. Create a moment that she'll never forget such as surprising her with dinner with some romantic music playing in the background. Play some Smokey Robinson over a plate of spaghetti and meatballs to warm up to the bedroom. It doesn't matter if she likes Smokey or the Italian entrée. She'll be appreciative of the effort and your sense of romantic adventure.

For the wife: The bedroom is a love domain. Set the stage of arousal to seduce your husband straight out of his work clothes. Look sexy for him by wearing some wonderful lingerie and a silk robe! Make him forget about his day at work. He may walk in the house and start complaining, but once he sees you for the sexy lady that you are, he'll easily switch his tone: "Oh my! Yes, indeed, woman, you look good!"

No money down and no down payment. These memories will last for a lifetime. Please don't overdo your creativity—sometimes it's the simple things in life.

<u>Day 25: Be a Creative Couple.</u>

Tips for Day 25
1. Marriage is the land of the living not the dead.
2. Marriage is the door and romance is the key.
3. The best gifts don't cost money.
4. Flowers, music, and dancing. The quality outweighs quantity.
5. Don't know how to be romantic? Google it.

Your Tips for the Day

Day 25: Be a Creative Couple.
Notes for your marriage_____

Day 26: The ten commandments of marriages.

This Book of the Law shall not depart from your mouth, but you shall meditate in it day and night, that you may observe to do according to all that is written in it. For then you will make your way prosperous, and then you will have good success (Joshua 1:8).

When the children of Israel left Egypt, they were about to experience a new way of living. It was a huge life-changing experience for them to go from slavery to freedom. To survive as a slave in Egypt there were rules for them to live by. Now there must be rules for them to live by as free people to keep their freedom. The same is true of marriage.

When you were single and bound by the slavery of the nightlife, there were rules you had to live by. For example:

a) Don't bring men home on the first night.
b) Believe nothing a guy says in a club because he's probably drunk.
c) Watch out for the easy women.
d) Don't drink and drive.

Now that you are married, you're free from the single life rules because you can't and don't live like that anymore. God gave the children of Israel the Ten Commandants to live by and to be successful in their new lifestyle. Marriage is the same. Every couple should have at least ten rules to live by and obey.

Day 26: The ten commandments of marriages.

Each person should make a list of five marital laws. And these laws cannot be broken at any cost. If these laws are broken—even one of them—the other mate will pay dearly for his or her transgression of the law. These laws should be written on your hearts and minds. Husband and wives need to get together and talk about five things each that they just can't and will not tolerate in their marriage. For example:

The wife, first:

1. When taking a bath, wash the bathtub out before you leave the bathroom.
2. Keep my car gassed up. I do not want to stop and get gas.
3. Put all your dirty clothes in one place and one pile.
4. If you're the last one out the bed, then make the bed up.
5. Do not take off your shoes (stinky feet!) in the dining or living room. (I don't want you to contaminate my aroma in the kitchen!)

Now the husband:

1. Read the tags on my clothes before you wash them.
2. Come to bed at least four out of seven days looking sexy (not just when you what to play baseball).
3. Stop telling me 347 times in one day to do the same thing.
4. Keep our house clean.

Day 26: The ten commandments of marriages.

> 5. Do not burn my chicken. And I am tired of taking the battery out of the smoke detector.

Now wasn't that oodles of fun? Makes you feel like you are getting some things off your chest. Obviously, these aren't the truest ten commandments, but they do help you both to focus on the little things in marriage.

Day 26: The ten commandments of marriages.

Tips for Day 26
1. You can't live by the singles commandments.
2. New stage in your life means new rules in your life.
3. Each person gets five commandments.
4. These are non-negotiable.
5. Remember what happened to the children of Israel when they broke the commandments!

Your Tips for the Day

Day 26: The ten commandments of marriages.
Notes for your marriage

Day 27: Evaluate your marriage.

Examine yourselves as to whether you are in the faith. Test yourselves. Do you not know yourselves, that Jesus Christ is in you?—unless indeed you are disqualified (II Corinthians 13:5).

It's a wonderful idea to review your marriage at least once a month. Take your wife out to eat at a nice quiet place and talk about last month. Ask lots of questions such as: How are you feeling? What is on your mind? Talk about what's going on in the marriage. Check on goals you made last month and possibly last year. At dinner, talk about what and how you're going to do things differently. Create a system for yourself and stick to it. Find different restaurants. Try different foods. Enjoy yourself and your mate.

This shouldn't be a business conversation. Talk about interesting and random topics like how insightful this book is and how you can't wait until I come out with another one. The reason it would be a good idea to do it monthly is because life happens so fast in marriage. You have children, battling in-laws, handling school, and tons of bills; all of this can zap a month into a year in real time. You can be together at church one month and in the courthouse the next month. Don't let the speed of life disrupt your marriage. Slow it down. Evaluate the moments and unexpected events will shine a light on things hidden in the dark; thus allowing you more control and a better sense of order, so you won't feel too overwhelmed. Dinner this would be a good time to ask all the questions that are on your mind—not on your way to your mother's house. This is good also because the wife

Day 27: Evaluate your marriage.

knows that once a month she will be able to vent. Now, this does not mean that there won't be any questions and venting during the weeks leading up to the date, but it will make it easier to handle. This is just letting her know that she is very much appreciated; you will listen to all that she has to say at dinner, and you look forward to this every month. Don't worry, husbands, this dinner swings both ways. The man will get his time to share his perspective on things as well. The more experience you both get from your monthly dinner time, the more your marriage will be strengthened.

<u>Day 27: Evaluate your marriage.</u>

Tips for Day 27
1. Every day your marriage should be going forward and not backward.
2. Create checks and balances for your marriage.
3. Don't wait too late to understanding the speed of marriage.
4. I recommend monthly dinners, but adjust for your marriage (once a week, once every two months, etc).
5. I hope this is not the only time you have dinner together.

Your Tips for the Day

Day 27: Evaluate your marriage.
Notes for your marriage

Day 28: Marriage Is Chess Not Checkers.

A wise man will hear and increase learning, And a man of understanding will attain wise counsel (Proverbs 1:5).

Marriage is very good because God made it that way. If you experience problems with your marriage, note that this is not the marriage—it's you and your loved one. One thing about marriage is, you must be creative. If you talk to single people, they would tell you how much fun they're having. Do you know why single people think they're having so much fun? Because they are doing things and meeting different people. Being married, you can do the same. You don't have to have an everyday routine with your mate. Go out and do different things with your spouse. Meet other married couples, hang out, and have fun. I think a married couple's life can be far more exciting than a single person's life. For one, there are more things to do as a married couple than being single.

What?

I am not going to tell you. Because I want you to use your creativity. Besides, I don't know your mate like you do. There are many different factors in this: what type of person your mate is, what city you live in, etc. Learn your city, get out there and live it up with your spouse. Don't wait for Friday night to come and sit around the house wondering what to do. Make plans for the weekend or whenever both of you can be together. If your marriage struggles, it's because you struggle as mates. Since you are married everything is legitimate—sex, kids, love, money, and a true friend (your mate). When you were single you could not trust any of these things.

Day 28: Marriage Is Chess Not Checkers

Read magazines, look at the Travel Channel to see where you can go. Do something other than watching ESPN or Lifetime, all day. Find things for you and your spouse to do in and out of the city. Take the children sometimes and leave the children sometimes. Use your head to create life-telling stories and dreams for your mate. A marriage goes forward not backward. You and your mate are getting older, not younger. Create great memories so you can look back and laugh at them. This is chess, not checkers means marriage is thinking and doing.

<u>Day 28: Marriage Is Chess
Not Checkers</u>

Tip for Day 28
1. Get creative in your marriage.
2. Think about the other person before you do things.
3. Make plans together.
4. Spend your time making the right moves.
5. Remember this is *'til death do you part*.

Your Tips for the Day

Day 28: Marriage Is Chess Not Checkers
Notes for your marriage

Day 29: Can I do all these things?

I can do all things through Christ who strengthens me (Philippians 4:13.)

Can I do all these things? That is a question that only you can answer. I can tell you physically and mentally, you can do all these things and more. The question shouldn't be *can* I do all these things? It should be *will* I do all these things?

I am sorry that you were never told that marriage is more than love. If all we need is love, then why are so many people getting divorced? You can ask a person who has been divorced before, and he or she would tell you "love had nothing to do with it." He or she just couldn't get along with his or her mate anymore or he or she did something to offend them. Whatever the case may be, love is innocent. People are guilty.

Marriage is hard work. Check your marriages for the weakest link. Find it and fix it. Don't look at divorce as an option, but every problem as an opportunity to correct something. There is nothing in this book that you can't do. There is nothing in your marriage that you can't do. It's never too late to fix and strengthen your marriage. People who file for divorce are weak in their marriages (not as a person). They feel like all their strength is gone and enough is enough. They just can't take it anymore. Just as a person that goes to the gym and works his or her muscles, marriage takes work. If you stop exercising your muscles, you will lose your strength. If you stop exercising the things in your marriage, your relationship will be weak.

Day 29: Can I do all these things?

When people get a divorce, it's a sad day for humanity. Giving up on your marriage is giving up on yourself.

Day 29: Can I do all these things?

Tips for Day 29
1. In marriage, there is only one place of no return (divorce).
2. Every marriage still has a chance.
3. You're not tired of your marriage; you're tired of your mate.
4. Find the weakest link and strengthen it!
5. Don't give up on your marriage; sometimes these things only come around once.

Your Tips for the day

Day 29: Can I do all these things?
Notes for your marriage

Day 30: Where is God in my marriage?

The eyes of the Lord are on the righteous, And His ears are open to their cry (Psalm 34:15).

Where is God in my marriage? That's a good question! After seeing the two of you together, I was wondering the same thing.

Short answer:
God's home is in heaven and earth is his footstool. Man is his creation and is made in his image and likeness. I guess you are still waiting for me to answer your question Where is God in my marriage?

God is a spirit and is everywhere at all times. The Bible tells us that God lives in us and around us. God is full of love, joy, peace, and righteousness. The Bible also tells us that God is always watching us (people).

God ordained the first marriage and gave man his first wife. God is love. He did not let Adam and Eve divorce. He did not let the snake destroy their marriage. He gave them Godly counseling and instruction on how to let nothing come between them. Oh, I am sorry I still didn't answer your question.

Where is God in your marriage?
If you believe everything I just said, and by the way it's all in the Bible, when you and your mate are in the house raising hell, saying and doing all types of evil things to each other, God is right there, watching and listening.

Day 30: Where is God in my marriage?

Tips for the Day 30
1. You can't be right with God and wrong in your marriage.
2. God hears and sees what you're doing.
3. Man looks at the outward appearance, but God looks at the heart.
4. God has given you his spirit.
5. You can WIN!

Your tips for the day

Day 30: Where is God in my marriage?
Notes for your marriage

Day 31: Entertainment.

And do not be conformed to this world, but be transformed by the renewing of your mind, that you may prove what is that good and acceptable and perfect will of God (Romans 12:2).

What are you doing? What are you watching and hearing on TV and radio? Do you know this stuff can have a big effect in your marriage? That's especially true if somebody's immature. Maturity has nothing to do with age or gender. Maturity is learning from experiences, and if you don't have any maturity, you better find some. What types of shows are you watching on TV? Are the shows you're watching encouraging and educational to your marriage? Are they well-rounded shows that give you ideas about things to do with your spouse? Or shows that teach you how to lie, cheat, and steal from your marriage? What do you think about the characters on the shows? Do you secretly like their rebellious attitudes and actions? Do you look at their lives and wish it were yours? Do you look at their mates (if they have any), wishing you were married to them?

Husbands and wives, you can't trust everything you see on TV. The role they're playing is not real. It's all about the ratings. Entertainment has fooled millions into thinking that a reality show is true reality. It's not! These people on these reality shows are good and bad actors. I have counseled several people who I could have linked with a reality show. They're trying to act like the people they see on TV. I am not saying something is wrong with these shows, but they're not meant for art to imitate life.

Day 31: Entertainment.

Stop trying to be "The Real Housewives of the city where you live." Your marriage is not a TV show! Why would you look at TV and fantasize about someone who doesn't fantasize about you? All your attention should be for your special someone.

Why?

Because your spouse is the one you're married to. Look at it this way: If you get sick or laid off from work, who has your back? Actors? Actresses? Who is going to bring you soup when you're sick? Tom Cruise? 50 Cent? Who is going to rub your body down? The people on TV? NO! When all else fails, you have your mate. Be smart and see the people on TV for what they are: entertainers.

Day 31: Entertainment.

Tips for the Day 31

1. Reality TV shows are not reality.
2. After watching a movie, leave the actors at the movie theater (don't bring them home).
3. Marriage is not a TV show.
4. You are a horrible actor or actress. (Your spouse e-mailed me and told me to put this down.)
5. If you want to act, why don't you act like a husband or wife and mother or father to your bad kids?

Your Tips for the Day

Day 31: Entertainment.
Notes for your
marriage

Conclusion

Marriage is a commitment to God and man. To fail in your marriage is to fail in the plan of God that he has for marriage. God builds family around marriage. To leave your mate should not be as easy as leaving a job. Marriage is a relationship to develop, not a job to work.

You may contact Dr. Tony Lester for a workshop, seminar, special event, or speaking engagement at www.rushhousepublishing.com
Visit Dr. Lester on www.facebook.com/dr.tlester
www.twitter.com/drtlester

www.ingramcontent.com/pod-product-compliance
Lightning Source LLC
Chambersburg PA
CBHW060834050426
42453CB00008B/685